Illustrations

CITY ON THE BLUFF

HISTORY and HERITAGE of MEMPHIS

By Rebecca L. Robertson

The Friends of Memphis and Shelby County Libraries

St. Luke's Press

Library of Congress Cataloging-in-Publication Data

Robertson, Rebecca, 1951-
    City on the bluff.

    1. Memphis (Tenn.)—History—Juvenile
literature.   I. Title.
F444.M557R63   1987   976.8'19   86-33853
ISBN 0-918518-54-7

Text and Illustrations: © Copyright, 1987, The Friends of Memphis and Shelby County Libraries

Funded by the Friends of Memphis and Shelby County Libraries
Additional Funding from Raccoon Books, Inc.

Book and jacket design by Susan Watters

ISBN 0-918518-54-7

To the Reader

This Memphis history book is the result of a collective effort on the part of many staff members of the Memphis/Shelby County Public Library and Information Center.

The book developed from an original idea of the History Department to create a slide history of Memphis for young people. After researching the available materials, it was decided to change the slide format to a video presentation. With the cooperation of the CIC Department, an 18-minute videotape called *City on the Bluff* was produced.

Because of the need for a written record of Memphis history, the Children's Department decided to compile a booklet based on the videotape. A drawing contest was conducted for students in grades four through nine to be used for illustrations in the booklet. The pictures that were chosen represented the young artists' impressions of the images they saw on the *City on the Bluff* videotape.

The Friends of the Library thought that the project was so worthwhile that they offered to fund the publication of a hardback book with colored illustrations. This created the need for a rewrite of the video text into a longer prose style. Monies were made available for the new text by a donation to the library by Raccoon Books, Inc.

City on the Bluff: History and Heritage of Memphis, consequently, is the result of contributions from many staff and nonstaff persons. We unfortunately can acknowledge only a few individually. Heather Tankersley coordinated the historical research and wrote the video text. David Carter produced the videotape. Ellen Baer and Jim Johnson proposed a written version of the videotape using illustrations by children. Judith Bennett and Betty-Erle Rhodes conducted the drawing contest. Angelo Omari and Hugh Spell contributed their artistic talents. Judy Card worked with the Friends of the Libraries to make the book become a reality.

We hope that the reader has as much fun discovering the history of Memphis as the staff has had researching and compiling it for this book.

1906
The first animal
in the Memphis Zoo
was a bear.

Bear: Lonnie Brown, Age 10
Parkway Village Branch

Have you ever stopped a moment in downtown Memphis and wondered how the city came to be what it is today? Little things might grab your attention. Have you ever wondered where the cobblestones on the riverfront came from? Why does downtown Memphis have such a mixture of old and new buildings? How did a park like Court Square get stuck in the middle of a bunch of skyscrapers and the hustle-bustle of a growing city?

The cobblestones, buildings and parks are just a few elements of the past still present in Memphis. Other remnants of that past can be found in names—the Hernando DeSoto Bridge, Tom Lee Park, Gen. Washburn Alley, and November the 6th Street. Where did the places in Memphis get their names? And the name "Memphis" itself is an oddity. Why was a city in the state of Tennessee named for a city in ancient Egypt?

Finding the answers to such questions will take you back to a time before those cobblestones, names, parks, and buildings existed. Memphis was just a bluff rising above a river. That river, of course, is the Mississippi, which means "great river." The river's name came from the Ojibwa Indians who lived near the Mississippi's source in the north.

If you use your imagination and do some detective work, you can find the answers to these and other questions. First of all, imagine Memphis without its bridges spanning the Mississippi River. Take away the buildings, businesses and houses, and even the crowds of people you're used to seeing.

If you think hard enough, you can erase all the things that presently exist and imagine just an elevated piece of land, covered with a wilderness of trees and vegetation standing above the changing flow of the river.

Now you can start your detective work. When you're involved in an investigation into the past, you can't search for fingerprints or look for evidence like a regular detective. You have to use clues from the past—maybe books, newspapers, old maps, letters, photographs, or stories from people who lived during an earlier time. Your "detecting" will trace the story of Memphis' history.

The Native Americans

The first people to live on the land where Memphis stands now were the Native Americans, the Indians. Since there are no written records of that time, even some of the best detectives can only guess at the date when they arrived. Archaeologists, the scholars who study prehistoric peoples, have found some clues about these people for us. They believe the Native Americans came to this area and established a string of towns along the river about 10,000 years ago—a time long before the great civilizations in Egypt and China.

The Native Americans lived in this area for thousands of years. Their life was based on hunting and gathering. Later, they began to cultivate crops, which allowed more people to live together in villages. As a detective, you can investigate how the Native Americans lived by visiting Chucalissa, an Indian Museum and village reconstruction. "Chucalissa" is a Choctaw word meaning "abandoned houses," referring to evidence that the villages along the Mississippi River were occupied, abandoned, and re-occupied several times during the period from 1000 to 1500 A.D.

European Explorers & Claims

The first historical or written clues we have of people being in the area we now call Memphis goes back only 445 years. That record came about when European explorers formed expeditions to search the "newly found" land they called America and some of the explorers kept journals describing their adventures.

The Spanish, French, and English were all interested in claiming land to gain control of the New World. They haven't left many clues in Memphis, but as detectives looking back at history, we can find evidence of their appearance in the area. Hernando DeSoto, the Spanish explorer for whom we've named the M-shaped bridge between Tennessee and Arkansas, found Native Americans living close to the Mississippi River near present-day Shelby County. After claiming the region for Spain, DeSoto and his band of explorers left.

Sometime shortly after the DeSoto expedition, the Chickasaws, one of many Native American tribes in the region, gained control of the area surrounding the bluff. They did not actually live in the place we call Memphis, but used the area as a hunting ground. The wilderness of that time was full of deer, bear, wolf, panther and buffalo. The Chickasaws were not just hunters; they also farmed and traded with the Europeans who were exploring the area. And the Chickasaws played an important role in the wars fought by the European adventurers seeking control of the region.

Although DeSoto may have been the first, he wasn't the only European explorer to claim the area for his country. The French and English also claimed the region. French explorers and traders, traveling from Canada and the northwest territory, were the next Europeans to encounter the Chickasaws. Father Jacques Marquette and Louis Joliet, who explored the region by traveling down the Mississippi River, passed by the Chickasaw lands in 1673. Nine years later Robert de La Salle camped on the Chickasaw bluffs when he traveled down the Mississippi River to reach the Gulf of Mexico. Exploring the "great river" was important to the French. They hoped to use the water route to connect their settlements in Canada and the upper Ohio Valley with the Gulf. They also hoped to stop the English, who were moving toward the Mississippi River from the eastern colonies.

During the nearly 200-year period when French and English explorers and traders were moving into the interior of America, the Chickasaws maintained control of the bluff region. They traded with both, swapping animal pelts for guns, beads, knives, tools, cloth, and other goods brought

Fort: Abhijit Kulkkarni, Age 10
Germantown Branch

by the Europeans. The Chickasaws adopted many European ways during this period. Since the Chickasaw domain included large areas of the southeastern United States, they were right in the middle of the struggle between colonists moving inland from the coastal areas of America—the English from the East, the Spanish from the South, and the French from Canada.

As a detective, you'll find records of this struggle. Those records will describe the first evidence of buildings in the Memphis area. When the French led expeditions against the Chickasaws in the 1730s, they built Fort Assumption on the fourth Chickasaw bluff. Historians believe the fort was located in the area of downtown Memphis. However, the French were forced to abandon the fort within a few months. Many of the Chickasaws helped the English during the French and Indian War, and after that struggle (1754-63), they were left in peace for almost 20 years.

Tennessee Becomes a State

The Revolutionary War kept the colonists in the East and the British and French too busy to pursue the Chickasaws. When that war ended and the United States had won its independence, the Treaty of Paris gave the state of North Carolina a claim to the bluff area. In 1790, North Carolina turned over control of present-day Tennessee to the United States, and the United States granted the region a territorial government.

Only a few traders lived in the bluff region; most Tennesseans were in the eastern and middle portions of the state. Spain was still trying to gain control of large portions of North America. Worried about American expeditions into the area, the Spanish built Fort San Fernando on the fourth bluff of the Chickasaws in 1795. The Spanish stayed in the fort from May to October, when Spain dropped her claims to the fourth Chickasaw bluff.

In 1796, Tennessee was admitted to the United States as the 16th state. Within a year, Spanish forces burned the stockade and left the bluff, taking anything of value with them. Although the fort was destroyed, it was the first building in the area that would eventually become Memphis and was located downtown between present-day Commerce and Sycamore streets. Troops from the United States moved into the region in 1797 and built Fort Adams, named in honor of President John Adams, on the site of Fort San Fernando.

The Chickasaw Cession & The Founding of Memphis

Feeling pressure from the growing number of colonists in the area, the Chickasaws were forced to give up the northern portion of their lands in 1818. The "Chickasaw Cession" opened up western Tennessee to settlement. The treaty with the Chickasaws was drawn up by two famous generals, Andrew Jackson, hero of the War of 1812 and the seventh president of the U.S., and Isaac Shelby, an officer during the American Revolutionary War and the first governor of Kentucky. The county in which Memphis is located is named for Shelby.

After the Chickasaws agreed to sell their land, a group of men bought claims so they could re-sell the land to settlers. These men, the founders of Memphis, were General James Winchester, a hero of the Revolutionary War; John Overton, a judge on the Tennessee Supreme Court; and Andrew Jackson, the general who helped negotiate the Chickasaw Cession.

It was Winchester who suggested the name "Memphis" for the city. Many American frontier settlements were named for the great cities of antiquity. Winchester was an educated man who was familiar with the classics.

He was also a soldier, and he had kept up with the events in Revolutionary France, particularly Napoleon's campaigns in Egypt. Winchester, who probably compared the Mississippi River to the Nile River in Egypt, proposed the name "Memphis" to help advertise the new city.

Jackson, Overton, and Winchester were developers and promoters. They never actually lived in Memphis. Although they are often given credit for "founding" the city, the actual settlers and the location of Memphis on the fourth Chickasaw bluff had more to do with the settlement's later success.

Tough Times for Early Memphis

The "city" of Memphis was laid out along the bluff frontage during April and May of 1819. Early Memphis was just four blocks deep and had a population of about 50 people. The first settlers were surrounded by wilderness and faced a difficult life in the fledgling city.

Other sites seemed more important then. Raleigh, (called Sanderlin's Bluff at that time), grew faster than Memphis in those early years. Memphis was also competing with another river town. Randolph, 42 miles upriver on the second Chickasaw Bluff, was a serious commercial threat in the 1820s and '30s. Also it was considered a healthier place to live than Memphis. The early settlers in Memphis suffered from bouts with various diseases in those early years. In 1836, the Randolph newspaper called Memphis "the great, grand fungus of the West."

You might think such problems would cause the end of the town. However, Memphis had a secret advantage which wasn't as clear in those early days as it is now. That secret was its location on a natural east-west crossroads. Old trails, left by the Native Americans, converged at the mouth of the Wolf River, which served as a crossing point to lands west of the Mississippi. Postal routes followed these trails, and in later years, the roads and railroads followed the postal routes. As these roads became more important than riverboat traffic, the success of Memphis was guaranteed.

Agricultural Growth & Slavery

The growth of Memphis depended to a large degree on the development of the land surrounding it. As that flat plain of rich land we call the Delta was turned into farm land, Memphis became a market for the farmers' products. During the first 15 years after the founding of Memphis, the land south of the city—in fact the whole northern portion of Mississippi—belonged to the Chickasaws. In 1834, the Chickasaws were forced to sell their remaining lands and move west. They followed a "trail of tears" through Memphis to territory west of the Mississippi River. The first group to leave was ferried across the Mississippi River from the Memphis landing on July 4, 1837.

Following the removal of the Chickasaws, northern Mississippi could be used for growing cotton. Even before the Chickasaw exodus, African-Americans had been brought into the region as slaves, and their importance as laborers was critical for the cultivation of cotton. By the mid-1800s, Memphis was the largest inland cotton market in the world, and the white fiber became economic king in the city.

Early Emancipation Efforts

Although most slaves worked in the cotton fields, some found work in the city as domestics, stevedores, blacksmiths, and craftsmen. Free blacks lived in the city, too. In fact, an emancipation society existed, supported by

Shelby County residents who favored eventual freedom for the slaves. The first mayor of Memphis, Marcus B. Winchester, encouraged his slaves to work for wages and purchase their freedom. He also advised and supported Frances Wright in her efforts to free slaves.

Frances Wright, a wealthy Scotswoman, was one of the most unusual women of her time. She made headlines wherever she went since she was in favor of economic and political reforms, women's rights, the abolition of slavery, universal public education, and religious freedom. She came to America to put her ideals of freedom and equality into action. For her utopia, or "ideal society," she selected a site 13 miles from Memphis on the Wolf River. "Nashoba," the Chickasaw word for "wolf," was the name she gave her 2,000 acre farm near present-day Germantown. Set up in 1825 as a farming community where slaves were educated and trained for freedom, the colony lasted only four years because of Ms. Wright's illness and financial problems. In January 1830, she sailed from New Orleans with the entire black population of Nashoba. The former slaves, 13 adults and 18 children, were resettled in Haiti.

How could slavery exist in a country that was based on ideals like equality, liberty, and the pursuit of happiness? Historical detective work reveals that slavery became an economic institution in the South because of its most important crop, cotton. By the 1830s, emanicpation was no longer regarded as practical. Tennessee even revised its constitution in 1834, taking away the few rights slaves did have and stripping free African-Americans of their citizenship rights.

The Growth of a City

Because of the increased agricultural production in the region,

Memphis became the most important city in the Mid-South area. A year after the founding of Nashoba, Memphis was recognized as a city by the state
government. Other events, which seem small to us now, are historical clues
that show us how Memphis grew. The city's charter was amended; a stage
coach line came through Memphis; the citizens founded an acting company;
a volunteer fire company was organized and the city's first fire engine, "Little Vigor," was put to use. During these years Eugene Magevney started one
of the first schools in the city. His schoolhouse was a log cabin on Court
Square. Magevney's Academy no longer stands, but his house at 195
Adams is Memphis' oldest surviving dwelling.

Early Memphis was often more like the western towns we see in
movies than a southern city. Citizens had to establish law and order. Instead
of the gunfighters of the wild west, the "bad guys" were the men who

worked on the rafts and flatboats along the Mississippi River. The "good guys" included William Spickernagle, the tenth mayor of Memphis, and the citizens who wanted law and order. However, the flatboatmen didn't want to obey the new laws. They also didn't want to pay the landing fees the city was charging. In 1842, the flatboatmen, led by a man named Trester (we don't know his first name), attacked the wharfmaster who had been sent to collect their landing fees. The wharfmaster escaped and returned with the

Hernando DeSoto: Ben Brents, Age 11
Parkway Village Branch

local militia and armed citizens of Memphis. Trester was killed and the flatboatmen were sent back to their boats.

As Memphis grew, the riverfront began to change. The cobblestones that make up the Memphis wharf were brought from Ireland to New Orleans as ballast, or stabilization weight, for the ships that had carried cotton to Liverpool, England. The stones were dumped at New Orleans and later brought up the Mississippi River in the slack season. Many miles of the rock are underneath the streets of Memphis, and the cobblestones now line the riverfront area.

The 1850s were a time of rapid growth for the city because of the merger of Memphis and South Memphis and the arrival of many immigrants. The Germans founded many of the city's businesses, particularly dry goods stores, clothing firms, and banks. Irish immigrants contributed to the city's growth as a railroad center. Many of them lived in "Pinch," a neighborhood north of downtown that no longer exists. The name "Pinch" came from the word "pinchgut," which was used to describe neighborhood residents who suffered from poverty and hunger.

Eugene Magevney, the famous schoolmaster, was of Irish origin. He made a fortune in real estate, became a political leader, and was instrumental in starting the city's public school system in 1848. Frank Monteverde, an Italian-American, was the first mayor of Memphis born in the city; the German Lowenstein brothers started one of the city's major department stores. A Frenchman, John Gaston, left his stamp on the city by donating five acres for a park. Today his name is recalled by John Gaston Hospital which was built with funds from his estate.

In 1857, a significant event occurred when the Mississippi River and the Atlantic Ocean were linked by the completion of the Memphis and Charleston

Railroad. Because this was such an important route across the South, many bloody battles were fought along the railroad's path during the Civil War.

The Civil War

Any detective searching for historical information about Memphis can discover the city's role in the Civil War. Memphis had ties to northern industrial cities because of the cotton trade, so many citizens wanted to stay in the Union. However, cotton planters depended on slave labor. Thus sentiment was divided at the outbreak of the war.

Before the mid-1840's, there was no commercial slave trade in Memphis. However, slave dealers started operating openly in the city in 1845. Most slave dealers had businesses in buildings along Adams Street. Historical clues about the slave trade in Memphis can be found in city directories from the period.

With the election of Abraham Lincoln, Memphians saw little chance for compromise with the northern states on the slavery issue, and by 1861 supported the decision to secede from the Union. Because the city had a good transportation network with the railroads and the river, Memphis became a military supply area early in the war. Like most members of the Confederacy, Memphians were confident of victory when the war began.

By February 1862, Tennessee's key defenses had fallen into Federal hands when Forts Henry and Donelson surrendered. Memphis served briefly as the state capital when Nashville was abandoned to the Union Army. In April, the Confederacy surrendered a strategic fortification at Island Number 10, which had guarded access to Memphis via the Mississippi River. And the Confederate defeat at Shiloh meant Memphis could easily be attacked from the east.

By the end of April, Union forces were attacking Fort Pillow, north of Memphis. The Confederate Army abandoned the fort in June, and the route to Memphis was open. As the Confederate troops retreated through the city, soldiers took what supplies they could carry, poured thousands of barrels of molasses down the riverbank, and set fire to some 300,000 bales of cotton on the riverfront.

On June 6, 1862, the Civil War came to Memphis when a small Union fleet defeated a Confederate fleet on the river in front of the city. Reports indicate that about 10,000 citizens stood on the bluff of the river to watch the battle. After the 90-minute naval battle, Memphis was in Union hands. Soon afterwards, General Ulysses S. Grant moved his headquarters to

General Washburn's Escape: Melissa Morgan, Age 11
Parkway Village Branch

Memphis, where he stayed in a mansion on Beale Street, now known as the Hunt-Phelan Home.

The most famous Memphian to cast his lot with the Confederacy was cavalry leader Nathan Bedford Forrest. Forrest's cavalry maneuvers gave hope to Memphians who supported the Confederacy. On the morning of August 21, 1864, his troops arrived in Memphis. Led by Nathan's brothers, Jesse and William, the Confederates rode into the city and almost captured three Union generals. William Forrest actually rode his horse into the lobby of the Gayoso House, a hotel on Front Street that is now part of Goldsmith's Department Store. One general was not at home, and the other two had enough time to escape. For General C. C. Washburn it was a close call. He was forced to run down an alley in his nightshirt. (You guessed it, detectives! That's where Gen. Washburn Alley got its name.)

Although Federal troops held the city, Memphis was the center of a smuggling network, furnishing supplies to the Confederacy. But Union occupation of the city meant slaves could no longer be sold. Blacks received not only their freedom, but also rights such as those of assembly and worship. Another new privilege was the right to read. The Freedmen's Bureau, established in Memphis in 1865, provided educational opportunities for blacks and protected their newly-won rights.

After the war, a large number of newly freed blacks came to the city from surrounding rural areas, but the citizens of Memphis failed to work for harmonious relations with the new citizens. In 1866, when some 4,000 black soldiers were waiting to be discharged at Fort Pickering, a three-day riot broke out between the blacks and whites in the area. To restore order, troops from Nashville were sent to place Memphis under martial law.

Although life in Reconstruction-era-Memphis was difficult and still unjust, blacks found their status much improved. The rights of assembly and worship were among their most-prized new freedoms. Blacks became active in fraternal and charitable societies, which played a key role in local political activity. One politically-active black, Ed Shaw, argued for integration and social equality. He led blacks to political victories in the 1870s, and Shaw himself was elected wharfmaster, a high-paying government office. Local ministers such as H. N. Ranklin, Africa Bailey and Morris Henderson built congregations and churches. Henderson's Beale Street Baptist Church was the most successful of these new churches, and the building can still be seen today.

Yellow Fever Epidemics

In addition to struggling with Reconstruction policies and race relations, Memphis was also struggling with disease. The city's growth was seriously handicapped during the late 1860s and '70s by yellow fever epidemics. In 1867, the same year that Memphis was designated the Shelby County seat, an epidemic of yellow fever struck 2,500 Memphians and caused approximately 550 deaths. The 1870s epidemics were even worse.

Yellow fever, a serious viral disease transmitted by the mosquito, got its name because in severe cases the victim's skin and whites of the eyes turned yellow. In the 1870s, no one knew the disease came from the mosquito. They blamed the outbreaks of yellow fever on filthy conditions in the city. In 1873, another epidemic killed 2,000 people. There was no known prevention or cure for the disease.

Despite repeated demands by citizens for a cleaner city, Memphis had no sewers, just gutters in the streets. These were the days before plumbing made bathrooms possible, and outhouses were often in the backyard, next to the water supply. The streets themselves were paved with wood which rotted. Gigantic mudholes threatened travelers in the city. During the late 1860s and 1870s, horses and mules (and sometimes the wagons they were pulling) regularly fell into uncovered cisterns, wells, and giant mudholes throughout the city.

Yellow fever struck Memphis again in late July of 1878. People panicked. Some 25,000 tried to flee the city, going in every possible direction. Many of them were already carriers of the disease. Every town and village within a 200 mile radius of Memphis imposed a quarantine against the fleeing Memphians.

Although many tried to escape, others stayed to fight the epidemic.

First School Bus: Kristen Green, Age 10
Parkway Village Branch

Doctors and other citizens tried to help during the emergency. The Howard Association, the Citizens Relief Committee, and the Catholic and Episcopal priests and nuns carried a large part of the burden, and many of them died when they caught yellow fever. Black Memphians, who suffered from the disease too, furnished many of the 3,000 nurses working under the Howards. They distributed supplies, comfort and care. In fact, blacks made up about 70 percent of the population that remained in the city and provided the work force for the community. They helped distribute $700,000 worth of supplies which poured in from all over the nation. They collected and buried thousands of corpses. Two black militia companies were formed to patrol the streets and prevent looting.

The yellow fever nightmare of 1878 ended with a mosquito-killing frost in October. Of the 20,000 citizens who had not fled the city, some 17,000 caught the fever and more than 5,000 died of the disease. Many who died are buried in Elmwood Cemetery, and Martyrs Park on the banks of the Mississippi River stands as a memorial to those who stayed and fought the disease.

Yellow fever nearly destroyed the city of Memphis. The loss of population from the epidemics, as well as a staggering $5 million debt, caused Memphis to lose its status as a city. In 1879, the state repealed Memphis' charter and placed the area under the control of the state, making Memphis a taxing district. Things looked grim for Memphis at that time, and the summer of 1879 brought another yellow fever epidemic. Although not as many people died during this attack, the epidemic increased the taxing district's financial problems. Memphis had a reputation as the least healthy place in the nation. Many out-of-town newspapers and some local citizens suggested that the site be abandoned.

Recovery, Growth & Diversity

As you continue your detective work on the history of the city of Memphis, you'll find the city had many ups and downs. Much of the evidence comes from the tales of war and disaster, like the story of the Civil War and the yellow fever epidemics. At other times, the evidence is harder to find—or it seems like a minor event. Such is the case when we start investigating the recovery of Memphis.

The first president of the taxing district was Dr. D.T. Porter, a druggist who became a businessman and developer. He worked to clean up the city. One of the first improvements was the installation of sewers in the city, and the Board of Health was given more authority to improve sanitation in Memphis.

The discovery of clean water was also important in improving health in Memphis. When the Memphis Water Company first started in 1873, it used murky-looking water from the Wolf River. Although the water was intended primarily for fighting fires and flushing sewers, many people drank it. However, in 1887 Memphians discovered the city was sitting on top of a vast underground water supply. Artesian wells provided billions of gallons of pure, clean water.

Gradually, the taxing district repayed its debts, and the state restored the city's charter and its power to tax in 1893. Memphis was once again a city.

A Return To Wealth

During this period, Memphis found its economic strength in cotton. Cotton was shipped up and down the river on steamboats, and it was not unusual to see the waterfront lined with cotton bales. The Memphis Cotton Exchange was established in 1873 to bring order and up-to-date information

to the local cotton market. Many of the commission houses were on "Cotton Row," located on Front Street between Jefferson and Beale, where they can still be seen today.

Some citizens, such as Napolean Hill, made fortunes based on cotton. Known as the "merchant prince of Memphis," Hill was involved in banking and cotton. He owned much downtown real estate and lived in an ornate mansion at the corner of Third and Madison where the Sterick Building now stands. Others among the rich and powerful were Noland Fontaine, a cotton investor, and James Lee, owner of a steamboat line. They lived in mansions we can still see in present-day Victorian Village.

Another rich and powerful person in Memphis during the late 1800s

27

was Henry A. Montgomery, a cotton merchant and president of the New Memphis Jockey Club, a horse-racing track located at Montgomery Park. At that time, Memphis was a horse-racing center. Fans could watch races at Montgomery Park and the North Memphis Driving Park. You can find evidence of these parks from maps of Memphis printed in the early 1800s. When Tennessee passed a state law outlawing betting, horse racing moved out of Memphis. The Park Commission bought Montgomery Park as a site for the regional agricultural fair. We know the park now as the Mid-South Fairgrounds.

The financial success of Memphis led to a building boom in the city. You can get a feel for the city's history by finding clues like postcards and photographs from the period as well as by visiting buildings that still stand in the city. One such structure, Cossitt Library, was built on the bluff over-looking the river. Established in 1888 with funds provided by the family of former Memphis businessman Frederick Cossitt, this red sandstone build-ing, which opened in 1893, was the beginning of the present public library system in Memphis and Shelby County. Another structure, the Porter Build-ing, was built in 1895 as the Continental National Bank Building. This 11-story building was the first skyscraper in the city. People came from all over and paid a dime for an elevator ride to the observation roof. The building was eventually renamed for Dr. D.T. Porter.

Economic Variety

Realizing the city needed more than the cotton industry to grow, Mem-phis merchants tried to develop and diversify the economy. The hardwood forests of the region were harvested, and lumber became the second most important product in the local economy. By 1900 there were more than 500 sawmills cutting down acres of trees in forests outside Memphis. Today we can see a portion of the wealth of the original West Tennessee wilderness in Shelby Forest.

Railroads continued to play an important role in the economy of Memphis. Until 1892 there was no bridge across the Mississippi River below St. Louis, mainly because the river was so much wider in the south. Railroad traffic which came to Memphis heading west had to stop, unhook cars, and ship them across the river on railroad ferry boats. The completion of the "Great Bridge of Memphis" was cause for a festive celebration in the city. At noon on May 12, 1892, some 50,000 people lined the bluff to watch as the world's third-longest bridge was tested by 18 steam locomotives hooked together. (Many were waiting for the bridge to fall.) Today we call it the Frisco Bridge.

By 1900, because of increased railroad use, steamboat traffic at Memphis was cut in half. Memphis itself had seen several riverboat accidents near its banks. In the winter of 1917-18, the *Georgia Lee* and the *DeSoto* were crushed by ice and sank near the foot of Wisconsin Street. Another boat tragedy occurred in 1925 when the *M.E. Norman* capsized. Tom Lee, a black levee worker who could not swim, rescued 32 people in his own small boat. A park on the riverfront where present-day Memphians enjoy numerous outdoor celebrations is named in his honor.

Improvements in the City

Economic diversification and the increase in transportation through Memphis meant the city was healthy and growing. One improvement made in Memphis at the turn of the century was an electric streetcar system. The new trolley helped Memphians move about the city, since it connected business and recreational areas, and led to the growth of residential areas which would later be absorbed by annexation into the city of Memphis. One such early subdivision was Lenox, which was created in 1890 and became a city in 1896. Lenox, which was bordered by Poplar, Central, Trezevant and Cooper, had its own mayor, developed its own water and sewer systems, and boasted the first fire-proof schoolhouse in the area. Memphis annexed Lenox in 1909, the same year the school opened. You can still see the Lenox School today, although it has now been converted to condominiums.

Photographs of Memphis streets at the turn of the century give us clues to how the city looked. In 1895, Union Avenue looked like a country lane. The now-bustling thoroughfare was only a tree-lined, dirt road. Other things we take for granted in modern cities were added in this period. General Sam T. Carnes brought several "modern" conveniences to Memphis. He introduced a Bell telephone franchise to the city in 1877, only a year after Alexander Graham Bell's successful demonstration of the new invention in Boston. He was also responsible for bringing electric lighting and the first automobile to Memphis. The speed limit was set at eight miles-per-hour to control these horseless carriages.

After annexing a huge chunk of land, city leaders began to establish a park system. When the city was originally laid out, the founders had donated a riverfront promenade and the downtown squares, including Court Square, as parks. As the city grew around them, these parks were reduced in size. In 1900, the city purchased two pieces of land. One at the northeast end of Memphis became Overton Park. The other, located at the southwestern corner of the city, became Riverside Park, now named Martin Luther King, Jr.-Riverside Park.

Church's Park & Auditorium, built by Robert R. Church, Sr., a millionaire black businessman, was the first park and entertainment center for blacks in the city. The six-acre park featured formal walks and gardens, a picnic area, playgrounds and a bandstand. The auditorium had a seating capacity of 2,000. Visitors like President Theodore Roosevelt and Booker T. Washington helped make Church's Auditorium an important part of life in Memphis. A generous and public-spirited Memphian, Church made large financial gifts to the city after the disastrous 1878 yellow fever epidemic.

A significant event in the early 1900s was the opening of the Memphis Zoo in 1906. The zoo's first animal was a bear abandoned by a baseball team and left chained in Overton Park. From that small beginning, our present-day zoo grew. An innovative step was made in 1914 when the first monkey mound was built. However, the ditch around the hill was not deep enough, and the monkeys kept escaping. In that same year, Memphis school children contributed their pennies, nickels and dimes to raise the money to bring Adonis Hippopotamus and his mate, Venus, from the Nile in Africa to the zoo here. Other Memphis Zoo animals have achieved fame and fortune, including Volney, the lion who roared for MGM movie openings before coming to the Memphis Zoo, and Memphis State University's mascot, "Tom the Tiger," who was donated to the zoo by an MSU football support group.

Race Relations

At the turn of the century, Memphis and other southern cities and states began to reduce the civil rights achieved by blacks after the civil war. During the racial crisis that erupted after a lynching in Memphis in 1892, thousands of black Memphians turned out for the funeral of the victims, but many fled the city in fear and despair. The black press fought back. One of the most vocal fighters was Ida B. Wells (later Barnett). Born in Mississippi and educated at Fisk University in Nashville, she became a schoolteacher in Memphis. As the co-owner and editor of the *Memphis Free Speech and Headlight,* she wrote an article opposing lynching and demanding that those responsible be punished. Forced to flee Memphis because of her stand, she continued her crusade against lynching from the North and from England. She never returned to Memphis, but her work helped bring the practice to an end in the South.

Laws were created to force blacks to sit separately on street cars, to exclude them from city parks and schools, and to reinforce residential segregation. These were known as Jim Crow laws, a term which was actually used before the Civil War to refer to racial separation on Massachusetts railroads.

Musical Magic

One bright spot for the black community was the legendary magic of Beale Street. Originally a residential street, Beale was transformed in the 1880s and 1890s to a street of restaurants, stores, offices, boardinghouses, and saloons. It was here that black ethnic music was popularized by William Christopher (W. C.) Handy as the "blues." Handy wrote one of his best-known songs, "The Memphis Blues," for Edward Hull Crump when he was running for mayor in 1909. It is believed that Handy composed this famous tune at Pee Wee's Saloon on Beale.

In the teens and twenties, Memphis was bustling with creative musical activity. As the leading blues artists of the day, Memphis singers and musicians spread their music to the rest of the country. Many people know about Handy's contributions, but few know that three of the best musicians in this period were black women—Alberta Hunter,

Lillian Hardin (Armstrong), and "Memphis" Minnie (McCoy).

Born on Beale Street, Alberta Hunter was a top recording and stage star. She performed in London and recorded many songs until she retired in the 1950s to care for her sick mother. Rediscovered in 1977, she became a star again and appeared on television numerous times before her death in 1984. Lillian Hardin (Armstrong)—a pianist, vocalist, arranger, and composer—was born in Memphis. She played on Louis Armstrong's *Hot Five* and *Hot Seven* recordings, and music historians give her credit for persuading her husband to form his own group. She died in 1971 while performing in a concert honoring Armstrong. "Memphis" Minnie McCoy mastered the banjo at age 10, bought a guitar when she was 15, and was discovered by a

Fontaine House: Clay Gillis, Age 11
Parkway Village Branch

record industry scout while she was playing on Beale Street. She was known as one of the best blues-jazz guitarists, recorded a number of songs in the 1930s and '40s, and died in Memphis in 1973.

The Crump Era

In the early 1900s citizens began to look for new leadership, and they found it in Edward Hull Crump, Memphis' most famous political leader. Nicknamed the "Red Snapper" because of his flowing red hair, Crump and his associates controlled city government for more than 40 years. As a detective looking back at Memphis history, you'll find numerous accounts of the importance of "Boss Crump."

Crump came to Memphis in the winter of 1894 with only 25 cents in his pocket. Within four years, he was the secretary-treasurer of a carriage company and was regarded as an up-and-coming business leader in the city. After his marriage to Memphian Bessie Byrd McLean, Crump took over the carriage business, made it the leading buggy company in the city, and achieved financial success.

For Crump, this was just the beginning. He became interested in politics. By 1902, he was in charge of the city's fourth ward. By 1910, he was mayor of Memphis and in control of local political power. Memphians voted for Crump for second and third terms, but he was ousted as mayor by the state supreme court. Even though he was not the mayor, Crump continued to control both city and state politics.

Medicine, Education & WW I

As a detective looking back at history, you've probably noticed that changes come to a city from both inside and outside forces. During the

1910s, medicine and education received a boost in Memphis from external forces. The University of Tennessee Medical School moved to Memphis in 1911, the same year the building of Baptist Memorial Hospital was begun. St. Joseph Hospital, founded in 1889, had grown into a 300-bed facility by 1919. These institutions, with the Memphis City Hospital and the facility that became Methodist Hospital in 1918, were the beginnings of the modern medical complex that exists in Memphis today.

The state's decision to locate a college near Memphis also helped make the city we know today. West Tennessee State Normal School, which opened at Buntyn (just east of Memphis) in 1912, eventually grew into Memphis State University. Although the college grew slowly at first, it prepared thousands of teachers who taught in the city, county, and Mid-South. Other colleges also helped improve life in Memphis. The two oldest institutions of higher learning in Memphis were LeMoyne College, which opened in 1870, and Christian Brothers College, which opened in 1871. Southwestern (now Rhodes) moved to Memphis from Clarksville in 1925, and S.A. Owen College opened in 1954. LeMoyne and Owen Colleges merged in 1968.

While Memphis was experiencing this growth, the world was going through the changes that led to World War I. The war would affect life in Shelby County. Many citizens entered the military, and the government built an aviation training station at Park Field near Millington. Although it closed after the war, this site would later become the home of the Millington Naval Air Base. Other wartime effects were indirect. The price of cotton soared, bringing prosperity to the region. The active involvement of women and blacks in the war effort altered their self-images and their positions in society.

Peabody Ducks: Melissa Morgan, Age 11
Parkway Village Branch

Social Changes

The women's suffrage movement, a campaign by women to achieve the right to vote, became increasingly powerful after WWI. The groundwork for this event had been laid much earlier. Elizabeth Avery Meriwether was one of Memphis' first advocates for women's suffrage. What's most remarkable about Ms. Meriwether is that she began her efforts shortly after the Civil War. In 1872, after reading that Susan B. Anthony had been arrested for trying to vote in Rochester, New York, Ms. Meriwether walked into the fifth ward polling place and filled out a ballot. Although she suspected it was never counted, it gave her a claim to being the first woman to vote in a United States election.

Ms. Meriwether continued to fight for women's rights in her newspaper, *The Tablet*. She spent her last years writing her memoirs, *Recollections of My 92 Years*. Although she did not live to see the enactment of the 19th Amendment which gave women the right to vote (she died in 1917), the U.S. Post Office issued a three cent stamp in her honor. In 1920 Tennessee became the 36th state to ratify the 19th Amendment to the Constitution.

Women's suffrage was just one of many social changes occurring in the United States after World War I. Blacks migrated to northern cities, and Memphis became a stopping point for many rural blacks moving out of the South. Richard Wright's story illustrates this pattern dramatically. He arrived in Memphis in 1917 at the age of 25. While working to save money for an eventual move north, Wright became an avid reader. A sympathetic white co-worker let Wright use his library card. By pretending he was just a messenger, Wright was able to check out books from Cossitt Library. Reading encouraged him to try writing. He left Memphis after less than two years and eventually became one of the greatest black writers in American history. The autobiographical novel *Black Boy* describes episodes from Wright's life in Memphis.

Blacks who stayed in Memphis had leaders in men such as Robert Church, Jr., a leader of the Republican party in Memphis and founder of the Lincoln League. The Lincoln League was important because of its success in registering black voters. Church also helped found the local chapter of the NAACP in Memphis in 1918.

One Memphian played an important role in changing the way Americans shop. Clarence Saunders was a leading businessman of the early and mid-1900s. He created a new way to sell food, the self-service store, when he launched his first Piggly Wiggly store in Memphis in 1916. The store was a success. By 1923 there were 2,600 stores nationwide and Saunders was a multimillionaire, allowing him to build the luxurious mansion we call the Pink Palace (now a science and history museum where you can see a model of the first Piggly Wiggly). Saunders made and lost three fortunes. One of his more innovative ideas was for an automated grocery store called the Keedoozle. By placing a key into a slot, the shopper could make a selection through a glass window. This process, although it didn't catch on in grocery stores, is very much like the vending machines you see everywhere today.

Overall, the 1910s and 1920s were years of progress. Detectives who examine this period will discover more clues that show how Memphis grew into the city we know today. During these years Brooks Memorial Art Gallery was built, the Pink Palace Museum was established, and the Orpheum Theater opened. All three events indicate Memphians were interested in art, entertainment, and culture. This was also the time when the Peabody Hotel first opened at its present location. Another sign of growth was the building of a second bridge across the Mississippi River. The Harahan Bridge, which opened in 1916, featured roadways for cars and trucks as well as railroad tracks. Between the time the first automobile arrived in the city and the time the municipal airport opened (1929), less than 30 years had passed and Memphis was becoming a "modern" city.

The Great Depression & WW II

The year 1929 marked another major event in the history of this country and the development of the city of Memphis. That event, the stock market crash of 1929, plunged Memphis and the country into the Great Depression

—a time of tremendous unemployment and financial suffering. Memphians tried to fight off despair by organizing a bit of frivolity. In 1931, after the price of cotton hit bottom, the first Cotton Carnival was held. The celebration was a success and became an annual event, one that is celebrated today as the Great River Carnival.

Once President Franklin Delano Roosevelt's relief programs were developed, the Memphis representatives in Congress, Senator Kenneth D. McKellar and Representative E. H. Crump, used their influence to bring federal projects to Memphis and Shelby County. The effects of the Depression remained in Memphis until the United States entered World War II in 1941. Because of its strategic location, Memphis developed into a military center. An air force depot, a supply depot, and the Second U.S. Army Headquarters moved to the area. The Naval Air Base at Millington was established in 1942, and in 1943 Kennedy General Hospital was opened on the southeast corner of the city. This $10 million hospital was located on a street with the unfortunate name of Shotwell, and Memphians decided to change the street's name to the more positive Getwell.

Other changes altered the look of Memphis and the lives of Memphians. After years of complaints about utility company charges for electricity, Memphians voted to join the TVA system in 1934, on Nov. 6. That's how November the 6th Street got its name. The city purchased the privately-owned power and light company in 1939, creating Memphis Light, Gas & Water. By 1945 and the end of the war, the economy in Memphis was in good shape. The price of cotton had doubled in five years, and the population of the city was increasing, creating a serious housing shortage. Construction began on another bridge to span the river by the Bluff City, and in 1949, the Memphis-Arkansas Bridge opened.

Mississippi River: John Ross McLoskey, Age 10
Raleigh Branch

John Ross McLoskey

Decades of Change

The recent history of Memphis has been filled with changes which have left their mark on the city. Many of these changes are still going on today and can be explored by reading your newspaper, watching television and listening to the radio.

In the 1950s, the city saw a number of changes. Named the nation's quietest, cleanest, and safest city, Memphis had come a long way from the mudhole that travelers on the Mississippi River described in the early 1800s and from its reputation as the "murder capital" of the nation at the turn of the century.

During the Depression, much of the downtown area had become

run-down looking. After WW II subdivisions sprang up, and the population sprawled out. Many of these changes are the result of the city's location. Because of the state line and the Mississippi River, the only way Memphis could expand was north and east. Responding to the shift eastward, merchants opened Poplar Plaza, the first shopping center in Memphis in 1949. It was a big success.

Urban renewal projects, which began in Memphis in 1957, also altered the look of downtown. In 20 years, 3,000 structures were demolished. Although renewal did eliminate some dangerous buildings, it also destroyed some historic landmarks and closed most Beale Street businesses. One exception is A. Schwab's, founded in 1876. Schwab's still has a turn-of-the-century flavor. The oldest operating general store in the mid-south, Schwab's offers visitors a glimpse into the past in its Beale Street Museum, which is filled with artifacts and memorabilia.

Musical High Notes

One of the more cheerful notes in recent Memphis history came from the music industry. In August 1954, Elvis Presley, a transplanted Mississippian, recorded his first songs, "Blue Moon of Kentucky" and "That's All Right, Mama." He went on to become an international celebrity and entertainer. After his death in 1977, his home, Graceland, became a major tourist attraction in Memphis. Millions of people have come from all over the world to view his gravesite and tour his home. Sun Records, a recording studio on Union, was connected with Presley as well as with such artists as Carl Perkins, Johnny Cash, and Jerry Lee Lewis. Stax Records, begun here in 1960, had contracts with such stars as Otis Redding, Muddy Waters, Isaac Hayes, and Rufus and Carla Thomas. They developed what became known as the "Memphis Sound" during the 1960s.

The Struggle for Equal Rights

The 1960s were years of struggle by black citizens for equal rights. After 1954, when the U.S. Supreme Court issued its decision against segregation in *Brown vs. Board of Education of Topeka,* black citizens actively sought civil rights. In the early 1960s, after an NAACP lawsuit, Memphis State University was successfully desegregated. LeMoyne-Owen College students began peaceful sit-ins and demonstrations at the public library. Eventually, buses, parks, museums, and other public facilities were integrated. The Memphis Committee on Community Relations (MCCR), a biracial organization, worked to achieve desegregation peacefully in Memphis. Black and white leaders also worked together in another area—politics. A new city charter was drafted, and Memphians approved it in 1966. The new charter eliminated the commission form of government and provided for a strong mayor to head the executive branch, with a 13-member legislative council.

Two years later, Memphis was again divided. Sanitation workers called a strike, in February 1968 to demand better pay and working conditions. Local NAACP leaders and black ministers backed the strikers and brought in the nationally-known leaders Roy Wilkins and Martin Luther King, Jr. The strike became a civil rights issue. King came to Memphis in mid-March and returned in April to lead a nonviolent protest march. The day after giving his "I've Been to the Mountain Top" speech, on April 4, 1968, King was assassinated on the balcony of the Lorraine Motel in downtown Memphis. Across the nation and in Memphis, civil disturbances erupted as some people expressed their grief, anger, and frustration. Although King's death was a tragic event, the assassination forced many citizens to re-evaluate their views on racial injustice.

Recent Years

The 1970s and '80s have brought increased growth in building in Memphis as well as increased interest in historic preservation and downtown revitalization. Detectives investigating this period will discover a boom in building. In midtown Memphis, the medical center complex was greatly enlarged as the University of Tennessee expanded and special hospitals such as Le Bonheur and St. Jude Children's Research Hospital opened. And there was a new excitement about sports—especially after the

Beale Street: Eric McNutt, Age 13
Bartlett Branch

opening of the Liberty Bowl Stadium and a new baseball park to go with the Coliseum, which had opened in 1964. As part of the nation's bicentennial, the amusement park at the fairgrounds was expanded in 1976 into the theme park Libertyland. Other areas of the city were also growing. William B. Clark built the high-rise White Station Tower, 10 miles east of downtown.

The continued shift in business patterns away from downtown convinced many Memphians to look for ways to redevelop the city's original business district. The Cook Convention Center, which opened in 1974, gave the city a new way to attract people downtown. In 1975, Main Street was converted to the Mid-America Mall, the longest pedestrian mall in the country. A growing public interest in historic preservation led concerned Memphians to work to save important buildings, including the homes on Adams Street now known as Victorian Village. Between 1982 and 1984, the Peabody Hotel, the Orpheum Theater, and Beale Street were restored and opened for business. Another effort to revive interest in downtown was the opening of Mud Island in 1982. The island, which began forming in the late 1800s because of shifts in the flow of the Mississippi River, had been a much-debated dilemma for Memphis since 1929. In fact, there were attempts to destroy the island because officials feared it would cut Memphis off from river traffic. None of the plans succeeded, and the island is now a river park.

Memphis has changed greatly from the time when artist Charles Lesueur visited the city and drew scenes of a primitive settlement in the 1820s. No longer is Memphis a mere cluster of cabins on the fourth Chickasaw bluff. The story of how it became the city it is today has taken us on a detective hunt through time. But there are many questions we haven't answered. Why was Thomas Edison in Memphis in 1865-66? When and why was the Hebe Fountain put in Court Square? Who is Ashburn-Coppock

Park named for? What's the oldest commercial building in Memphis? Where are distances measured from in Memphis? Where and what is the Amasis Stone?

These are just a few questions we haven't answered in our investigation. You may have more of your own. To find the answers, you'll need to search for clues. Looking for clues to a city's history isn't always easy, but it doesn't have to be hard work either. You'll find some clues by actually visiting places in Memphis. Others are on historical markers standing in the city. You can ask older people to describe life when they were growing up. You'll find a wealth of information at your neighborhood library, and serious detectives can find even more in the Memphis and Shelby County Room at Main Library, a resource on the history and heritage of this region. Traces of history are all around us. In Memphis, you'll find a rich combination of the past, present, and future in day-to-day life. Many puzzles are still here for historical detectives to solve. Start your own investigation, and happy sleuthing!

This is a black officer
during yellow fever epidemic.

Black Officer: Elizabeth Duckworth, Age 11
Parkway Village Branch

Friends
Of Memphis Shelby County Libraries

The Friends of Memphis and Shelby County Libraries is a non-profit organization of citizens working together to support and enlarge the scope of public library service in Memphis and Shelby County.

Friends believe in public libraries as vital centers of communitcation, centers that are necessary to provide people with the information they need to understand the complex issues of the modern world. They encourage the use of the library as a center for the cultural and civic life of the community.

They also believe in the freedom to read and the value of books and reading. They endorse the stated philosophy and objectives of the Memphis/Shelby County Public Library and Information Center.

Friends provide direct financial assistance by purchasing special items which are of great benefit but cannot be purchased from the library budget. Friends' funding also supports the West Tennessee Talking Library, the Community Information Channel, and the Memphis/Shelby County Room.

The Friends work to create public support for an expanding library program. They aid in public relations by informing the community about the library's services, and through their affiliation with the American Library Association, they work for library legislation and appropriations.

1850 Peabody Avenue
Memphis, TN 38104
Phone 901 725-8852